Spaces and Places:
Views of Montgomery's
Built Environment

1. *Vandepoel Electric Railway at Court Square*

Spaces and Places: Views of Montgomery's Built Environment

May 13 through July 9, 1978

Montgomery Museum of Fine Arts
Montgomery, Alabama

This exhibition has been funded in part by a grant
from the Alabama State Council on the Arts
and Humanities.

Montgomery Museum of Fine Arts
440 South McDonough Street
Montgomery, Alabama 36104
(205) 834-3490

Printed in the United States

CONTENTS

Throughout history, art and architecture have been profound influences on the quality of life within a community. Art museums, sensitive to the unique relationship which exists between both disciplines have mounted numerous important architectural shows in the past decade. The Corcoran Gallery presented a major exhibition of the visionary work of architect Paolo Soleri. The Columbia Museum of Art in South Carolina featured the work of Robert Mills, the first American to prepare for a career as an architect. Numerous exhibitions have been presented illustrating the architectural history of cities in Wisconsin, New Jersey, and New York.

Montgomery, Alabama is especially rich in its architectural heritage. Fine examples of Greek Revival, Italianate, and Queen Anne architecture exist throughout the city, and the current exhibition illustrates many examples from approximately 1830 to 1900. This is the first exhibition of its kind to be presented at the Museum. Four sections in the downtown area have been selected as areas of concentration: Capitol Hill, the Commercial District, Court Square, and Residential areas. Geographically, architectural examples are represented within the area bounded by the Martin Luther King Expressway, Jackson Street, and the Alabama River.

The exhibition was directed by Diane J. Gingold with the assistance of a dedicated committee who participated in its organization. All must be commended on a splendid effort.

Henry Flood Robert, Jr.
Director

Like the outline of Montgomery which is a composite of architectural signatures, this exhibition is the result of a combination of ideas and efforts. First, I would like to thank the committee who devoted endless hours of their time to work on the multitudinous details: Tom Blount, Ellen Mertins, and Mary Ann Neeley provided the architectural and historical background; the expertise and knowledge of museum needs and requirements that enabled us to adapt the city's architecture to the museum structure and interpret it to the museum visitor were provided by Katherine Campbell, Barbara Redjinski, and Ronald Roth.

Because this exhibition must, by its very nature, extend beyond the museum's walls, two publications were written. This catalog provides the architectural history and perspective of the selected structures; the accompanying self-guide by Ron Roth, Alabama Museums' Coordinator, takes the visitor outside the museum and is the vehicle for heightening an individual's awareness of the architectural art that surrounds him. Like the exhibition, the catalog could not have been completed without the assistance of many individuals. I would like to thank Milo Howard, Director of the State Department of Archives and History for his enlightening introduction, Ellen Mertins and Mary Ann Neeley for the introductory essays for each section, Donna Hole for her entries on the State Capitol and commercial buildings, and Katherine Campbell, assistant curator, for her invaluable assistance preparing the completed manuscript. I would like to especially thank Lou and Julie Toffaletti for the excellent catalog design.

The installation of the exhibition is comprised of two parts—the photographs and the architectural fragments. Photographs were culled from a variety of sources, some dating as far back as 1894. For this visual record, I would like to thank June and John Scott who not only provided the contemporary photographs, but whose comprehensive library of negatives was the source of many interesting older photographs, and Barbara Redjinski who took many perceptive detail photographs. Tom Blount located the architectural fragments used in the exhibition and helped plan the installation. Most importantly, I appreciate the assistance of the entire Montgomery Museum of Fine Arts Staff—in particular, Ted James for the installation and Patti Mastin for her patience in retyping the many manuscript drafts. Likewise, I would like to thank the Alabama State Council on the Arts and Humanities for providing an essential grant. In addition, I would like to acknowledge the many other individuals and organizations who lent works to the show and showed enthusiasm for the project.

Finally, I thank all the known and unknown architects of the past that have made the City of Montgomery the delightful architectural phenomenon it is.

Diane J. Gingold
Curator

INTRODUCTION

The ambitious hopes of the founders of Montgomery are still evident in the old part of the city even after more than a century and a half. Indeed, the constant growth of the town has caused building and rebuilding over the same ground generation after generation; but the basic plans of New Philadelphia and East Alabama, the parent towns, laid out in the frontier wilderness in 1817 and 1818, are unchanged. Andrew Dexter envisioned New Philadelphia as the future state capital. Toward that end he reserved the most prominent hilltop in his town as the site for the future state house, and leading to it he laid out a broad avenue as its fitting approach. The rival land company, which recognized the suitability of the bluff on the Alabama River as a commercial town site, laid off a town with streets oriented to the river. Through its center and connecting with Dexter's Market Street ran the almost equally broad Commerce Street. Whether by design or by accident, the basic plan of the old city thus acquired a baroque character with intersecting broad avenues forming odd-shaped parks and squares with broad, open spaces.

When New Philadelphia and East Alabama were combined into one town and made the county seat in 1819, the largest of the intersections, created by Commerce and Market Streets, was chosen as the site of the courthouse. When the new, forty-foot square, two story building was erected in 1821, it stood in the midst of a town of 81 structures, 17 of two stories, 32 of one story, and 38 log cabins. Soon, a few brick buildings were built, the first reputedly being Freeney's Tavern on Commerce at Tallapoosa, where the Marquis de la Fayette was entertained in 1825. By 1871, Matthew Blue, Montgomery's first historian, was complaining nostalgically that the old tavern was being demolished. But even earlier, as Montgomery prospered and grew, the old, original buildings were pulled down to make way for newer, more handsome, and more commodious structures. Even as early as 1834, the Courthouse was rebuilt, this time in brick but on the site of the original in what had already become known as Court Square.

Radiating from the Courthouse, Commerce and Market Streets remained the center of town like a broad, bent axis. The Montgomery Hall at Lawrence and Market and the Exchange Hotel on the square became, upon construction, the town's finest buildings and were soon joined by the Winter Building. Lesser, two story brick buildings began to line the main streets while cotton warehouses grew up near the river. Unquestionably, the courthouse square was the center of town and the appropriately named Commerce Street, running

from it to the river, was the scene of business activity.

The selection of Montgomery as the State Capital in 1846 had a dramatic effect upon every aspect of the city, which soon became apparent in its appearance. The land at the head of Market Street had been available for a quarter of a century, and Montgomerians immediately subscribed a $75,000.00 bond issue to build the Capitol. Stephen Decatur Button, one of the leading architects working in the South, was engaged by Montgomerians to design a suitable building which was completed in November, 1847. The pride of the city was thus expressed in its architectural gift to the state. The presence of the Capitol had an almost immediate influence upon other construction in the city. Down came wooden church buildings, and in their places brick and stucco edifices rose. The frame buildings still standing on Commerce and the lower end of Market Street soon fell to the optimism of the promoters of the city, who also rebuilt their own homes on a much grander scale, some in the Greek Revival style but most in the more popular Italianate style.

The destruction of the Capitol by a disastrous fire on December 14, 1849, gave Montgomery pause while the Legislature debated whether to rebuild in Montgomery. In the meantime, space for the use of the Legislature and the Supreme Court was available, and readily offered, in the hotels and in the assembly rooms, Estelle and Concert Halls, on the second floor of the newly constructed brick buildings on the north side of Market Street at Lawrence. The decision to rebuild the Capitol in Montgomery allowed for modifications in the original design which made the dome a more commanding feature of the structure than the more classically proportioned dome of the Stephen Button building had been. The unpedimented portico of the new building, also providing a place for the new city clock on the building, enhanced the street-level perspective of the building from one end of Market Street to the other.

Led by the expanding city, Montgomery County grew, and that growth required still a larger courthouse. Abandoning Court Square, the county government moved to Washington Street at Lawrence, while the city embellished the old well on the square, creating a fenced area known as "The Basin." Even without the courthouse, the Court Square remained the commercial center of town. In the 1850s, the Central Bank Building was constructed at the corner of Market and the square. Belshaw's corner at Commerce and the square and the buildings fronting the Basin dominated the city's business and commercial district; but business was expanding, moving first into Monroe Street and then to the streets crossing Market and Commerce. The residential area began also to move up the inner slope of the ridge of hills surrounding the town, giving way for more, larger, and better constructed commercial buildings.

In spite of its growth, Montgomery was not prepared for her moment's glory as a nation's capital. The organization of the Confederate government in the State Capitol in February, 1861, found the town's hotel facilities inadequate. A small town atmosphere emanated from the unpaved and irregular streets in spite of Montgomery's pretensions based upon recent construction. The fact that the Confederate government building at the corner of Commerce and Bibb Streets was less than two blocks from the presidential residence at Lee and Bibb indicated both the constricted area of development and the indiscriminate growth of the city. To those accustomed to Washington, the town was unquestionably provincial.

The War Between the States and Reconstruction ended the building boom of the 1850s. As the city began its slow recovery late in the Reconstruction period, the first City Hall was erected on the site of the present city building. Government had already become the basis of stability in Montgomery. The Capitol, dominating the city from its eminence at the head of Market Street symbolized the fact. The City Hall underscored it. New construction on Commerce Street heralded the economic resurgence of Montgomery as the commercial center of central Alabama. Six railroads converging on the city within easy distance of the river wharf eventually resulted in the construction of a Union railroad terminal, which, along with the land, created a suitable terminus for Commerce Street.

The baroque character of the axial streets was completed with the erection of the Fountain in Court Square in 1885. That year saw also the enlargement of the Capitol by the addition of the east wing, the beginning of street and sidewalk paving, and the introduction of the street railway. Much of the architectural character of the city was set by 1890. Only the skyscraper remained for the 20th century. Belshaw's corner briefly supported the Second Empire style Moses Brother's Bank and a block away the old Masonic Temple was built in a similar style. Both were short-lived, and in their places rose the First National Bank and the Greystone Hotel. The historic Exchange Hotel with its Greek Revival columns fell victim to new construction methods and was replaced by the steel-framed new Exchange. Fires on Commerce and

Market (Dexter Avenue since 1885) necessitated further changes as did periodic bursts of economic growth. All such changes reflected the architectural tastes of the times, but no developments were so complete as to obliterate relics of earlier days.

Until the middle of the 20th century, business, commerce, and government were confined to the "downtown" area. Yet withal, the center of the city retained much of its character. The changing economic base and modern transportation modes broke the stranglehold of the downtown area and threatened the very existence of the historic center of the city. Only the ever-expanding government complex steadily grew as new office buildings were added on Capitol Hill.

Urban renewal changed some of the face of the downtown district, but here and there a building remains, which would be familiar to past generations. The Winter Building, with or without its balconies, the Central Bank, and the Fountain still dominate the square. Commerce Street from the river almost to the square has more than a few vestiges of the last century some dating even to *ante-bellum* days. The chimney pots at the corner of Perry and Dexter have been a part of the Montgomery horizon since the 1830s. Estelle and Concert Halls are thinly disguised behind new brick facings, but across the street a new bank stands upon the site of the Montgomery Hall, which already had given way in the 1880s to the Romanesque federal court and post office building. These are but a few examples. More remain than might be thought at first glance, for still interwoven in the structural fabric of downtown Montgomery is to be found the history of the growth of the city written in its architecture.

Milo Howard

019429. DEXTER AVENUE AND THE CAPITOL, MONTGOMERY, ALA.

2. *View of Dexter Avenue from Court Square*

For nearly a century, Hebe, the goddess of the fountain, has gracefully presided over Court Square as the most visible symbol of Montgomery. Located at the intersection of three major streets—Dexter, Commerce, and Court—the square has been the focus of business and social activity since the founding of the town. There, vendors of assorted merchandise and local gossips converged daily bringing with them an air of bustling life; auctioneers sold cattle, cotton, land, and, occasionally, slaves; and volunteers were mustered for the Indian skirmishes, Mexican conflict, and Civil War.

After the two rival settlements, New Philadelphia and East Alabama, put aside their differences and joined as Montgomery in 1819, the boundary between them was selected as the site of the courthouse. The focal point of the square facing the courthouse was the artesian spring later known as Big Basin. The rush of merchants and land-hungry settlers, following the vanguard of speculators, brought increasing prosperity and progress to the small community. By the late 1840s, the area around the square could boast a number of respectable buildings, including the notable Exchange Hotel and the beautifully proportioned Winter Building, skillfully designed in the then newly fashioned Italianate style.

Civic and social ambition was expressed in a concern for the appearance of the city, which was taken seriously lest a visitor from more sophisticated parts write home disparagingly. Men of means advertised their prosperity and taste by erecting business houses in the most fashionable styles; editorials and newspaper accounts frequently referred to buildings as "ornamenting" or "enhancing" a location. Consequently, when William Knox determined to erect a new structure to house his Central Bank (Klein and Son) in 1856, he called on Stephen Decatur Button, an eminent Philadelphia architect who had earlier designed the State Capitol and Knox's own home in the Greek Revival style. By this time, the Greek Revival was less fashionable, and Button and Knox selected an elaborate design based on Venetian palaces of the 15th century. Newspapers sparkled with praise for the new bank, and a few years later criticized the older, nearby Belshaw building for "not getting in line with the other beautiful buildings in the area."

When Montgomery became the state capitol in 1846, the city's population enlarged with the arrival of politicians and their followers. The Exchange Hotel, also designed by Button, became one of the most important meeting places for politicians in the state, and following the burning of the Capitol, served as the seat of government. In 1861, when Montgomery hosted the Confederate government, the hotel on the square entertained Jefferson Davis, his cabinet, members of Congress, and frequently, northern and foreign newsmen.

After the turmoil of war and reconstruction subsided, attention again focused on the city's appearance. Streets were upgraded, sidewalks paved, and disdainful glances were cast on the old artesian well which now seemed an eyesore to those dazzled by the promises of progress and prosperity. Anxious to improve its image, the city commissioned one of its aldermen to find and buy a suitable fountain to ornament the central square. The fountain, cast by J. L. Mott Iron Works of New York, was every bit as exuberant as the period. When it was erected in 1885, it was immediately hailed as a "thing of beauty."

Court Square was unplanned; its present strong appearance accidentally emerged from the interaction of competition and cooperation. Ornamented with the central fountain, the square is securely flanked by the contrasting Winter and Klein and Son buildings. Nearby, the superb Montgomery Fair, the little mansard-roofed Maner Building, and the 1975 First Alabama Bank addition clearly express the stylistic influences of their respective periods. Change is inevitable. The fine vistas up Dexter and down Commerce have been altered over the years as each generation has attempted to impose its aesthetic ideals. The square, recently redefined and partially closed to automobile traffic, has lost some of its earlier buildings; but Hebe, long isolated in a sea of traffic, is once again accessible to the casual downtown wanderer.

KLEIN AND SON, 1856
1 Dexter Avenue

3. *Klein and Son*

In 1856, the *Montgomery Mail* reported the demolition of the old corner of Market and Court Streets in preparation for an elegant, modern structure with a cast iron front designed by S. D. Button, Esq., Architect, Philadelphia. William Knox, owner of Central Bank, hired Button who earlier had drawn the plans for the State Capitol and Knox's home. The building was designed in the fashionable Renaissance Revival style and utilized cast iron ornament to enrich the facade, a unique architectural element in Montgomery. Venetian palaces from the 15th century served as prototypes for the building—tall, arched windows, sculptural ornamentation, and a layering of wall surfaces illustrate the Italian influence as adapted to commercial structures.

The building incorporated a modern feature for its day, the use of ornamental cast iron around recessed windows. Contrary to the contemporary newspaper report, the entire front was not of iron; individual pieces of cast iron were attached to the masonry structure. This was an inexpensive means to simulate elaborate stone decoration. To achieve the appearance of stone, the building was painted. Here, the cast iron decoration is distinguished from the masonry by a different color paint. By the late 19th century, cast iron ornamentation had declined in popularity and was replaced by terra cotta and pressed tin.

The ownership of this building changed a number of times before being acquired in the 1920s by Klein and Son. After acquiring the building, renovations and alterations were made on the street level to accommodate their needs. The original street level windows, which were identical in shape to the second and third story windows still intact, were replaced by 20th century display windows.

BELSHAW BUILDING, c. 1830
8 Commerce Street

MOSES BUILDING, 1887-89
8 Commerce Street

FIRST ALABAMA BANK BUILDING, 1907
8 Commerce Street

The development of the corner now occupied by the First Alabama Bank has paralleled the growth of commercial architecture in America and has been the site of three prominent buildings. The first recorded building to occupy the site was the Belshaw building, a brick store constructed about 1830. The simplicity and utility of the design was typical of the earliest commercial buildings as was the parapet wall bridging the chimneys. A veranda with slender posts and curved trim provided the only ornamentation. In 1887, the building was demolished to make room for the "Great Moses Building."

The skyscraper style premiered in Alabama in 1888 with the completion of the six story Moses Building. It caused great excitement and people came from throughout Alabama to marvel at the building's dazzling height. Like New York skyscrapers of the late 19th century, it emphasized increased window area, but it retained the mansard roof and central tower of the earlier Second Empire style. Height was accentuated by tall vertical piers rising at two window intervals to the top of the fifth story. Also notable was the interior elevator, an exciting technological invention that enabled tall buildings to flourish.

Although considered advanced for its day, the Moses Building was nevertheless outdated at its completion because of new structural innovations developing in the Mid-West. The use of steel framing allowed architects to design buildings of a height not possible with masonry. Within 20 years, the Moses Building was demolished.

In 1907, the steel framed First National Bank which rose to a grand height of 12 stories was constructed for a cost of $300,000. Like many of the leaders of the new commercial style, the building's architects chose to emphasize its height. Despite horizontal bands at several points, the vertical strips of windows dominate.

Terra cotta decoration was a common feature of the commercial style and appeared in this building in the ornate lion heads which have been removed. Nearby, the Bell Building on Montgomery Street makes elegant use of the same material.

4. Belshaw Building

5. Moses Building

6. First Alabama Bank Building

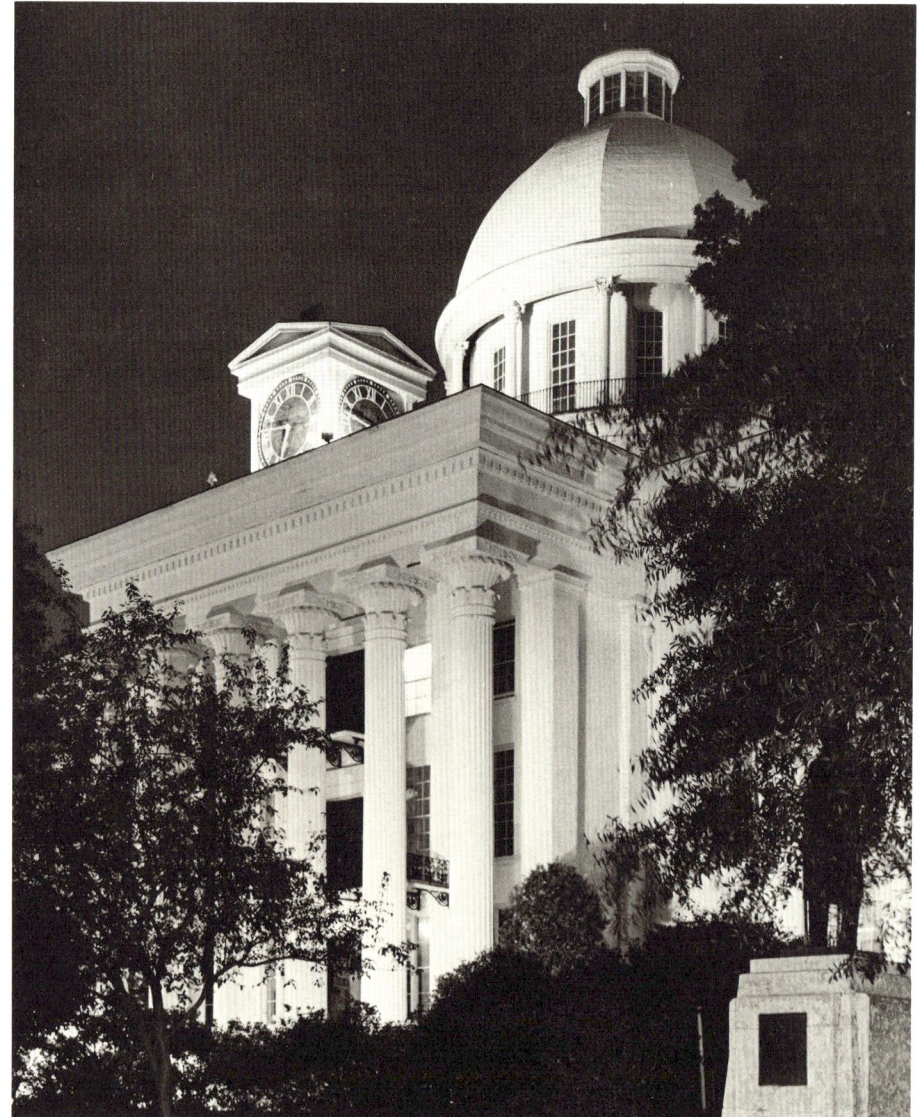

7. *State Capitol Building*

Rising from a hill at the end of a wide avenue, the Alabama State Capitol creates an unforgettable impression. This magnificent view was envisioned by Andrew Dexter in 1817 when he founded the frontier settlement of New Philadelphia. He optimistically foresaw his town as the future capital of the state and drew his plans accordingly. Possibly inspired by the broad streets and exciting vistas of L'Enfant's design for the national capital, he reserved the hill at the eastern end of the main avenue for a statehouse. Dexter's early vision was realized in 1846 when Montgomery became the state capital and the grassy knoll, by then known as Goat Hill, was donated as the site for the new capitol.

The first elegant Capitol was designed by Stephen Decatur Button who utilized motifs from Minard Lafever's *The Beauties of Modern Architecture,* one of the most widely used Greek Revival pattern books of the day. The Greek Revival style, popular in the first half of the 19th century, symbolized ideal democracy and was used for public buildings throughout the nation. This idea was embraced most heartily in the Deep South, where six of the state capitol buildings were designed as "temples of democracy." In 1849, Alabama's magnificent state Capitol burned and only portions of Button's plan— primarily the Lafever designs— were incorporated into the new building completed in 1851.

The upper end of Dexter had been the business district of New Philadelphia, but the rush to Court Square by the merchants in the 1820s almost vacated the area. The building of the Capitol and the ensuing governmental activities, however, did help to revitalize the section although it was never again a commercial center. Houses lined the street approaching the statehouse, the surrounding blocks, and even the southern end of the capitol square. Detracting from the many fine residences were the shabby parts of the main thoroughfare. By the 1880s, the *Montgomery Advertiser* was complaining about "wooden shanties" on the north side of Dexter under the very nose of the Capitol." Today, these and the substantial homes have given way to state buildings as government services and agencies have multiplied.

Although moved to its present location next to the state archives building in the 1920s, the White House of the Confederacy reflects the once residential character of the area and portrays urban living of the 1860s. Constructed in the 1830s at the corner of Lee and Bibb streets, the frame residence was updated in the 1850s and consequently exhibits stylistics elements from both periods. The interior design of the front rooms reflects the Federal period influence with paneled wainscot and delicately designed mantels, while the exterior has the bracketed cornice and low veranda of the Italiante style.

The availability of land on the upper end of Dexter was probably a factor when a black congregation acquired the site of a former slave market at the corner of Dexter and Decatur for their new church. In 1885, construction was begun on a substantial brick building by the Dexter Avenue Baptist congregation. When completed, the church was an eclectic blend of Gothic and Victorian elements and was typical of the urban churches of the period. Because the Greek Revival was strongly associated with the pagan religions of Greece, its suitability for churches had long been questioned. By the 1850s, the Gothic Revival, a more Christian style of architecture, had become the most popular for churches and remained so for the rest of the century. When the new church was completed, the Dexter Avenue Congregation immediately embarked on a campaign to raise money to locate the State Normal School in Montgomery, inaugurating a long history of social involvement in the community.

Historically, these three buildings are among the most significant in the nation, linked as they are to movements and specific events which have affected the entire nation. Two of them— the Capitol and the Church— have been officially designated as National Historic Landmarks. The third, the White House, has been listed on the National Register of Historic Places. Stylistically, each of these buildings was well suited for its use. The Greek Revival Capitol proclaimed its builders' belief in the democratic process and their hopes for its fulfillment; the refined Italianate elegance of the White House provided suitable living quarters, and the sturdy eclectic design of the church reflected the pride and independence of its congregation.

8. *Detail, State Capitol Building*

The Alabama State Capitol dominates the Montgomery skyline and subtly embodies over a century of evolution in architectural taste and method. When completed in 1847, the classically simple structure was planned to serve the needs of a young, sparsely settled state. As the state grew, the Capitol was able to expand gracefully without losing its architectural identify.

Stephen D. Button, an aspiring architect from the North, designed a Greek Revival building for Montgomery in 1846. Although this style was declining in popularity by the late 1840s, it continued in use in state houses because of the strong association with the democratic ideals of ancient Greece. Architects across the country, with an eye to the work being done on the national Capitol, had begun to combine the classical elements of the Roman dome and Greek temple forms with porticoes to create a style which had become almost a formula in capitol construction.

A tragic fire on December 14, 1849 completely destroyed Button's building. Construction began anew on the charred foundations in the spring of 1850. The building commissioners turned to local architects to rework the plans by Button, who was by now well established in Philadelphia. While retaining some of Button's elements, an unknown Montgomery architect altered the vertical proportions significantly. He changed the two-storied portico to three stories to accommodate higher walls and a lower basement level. The pediment, which is normally part of the portico, was omitted to provide a place for the city clock. However, Minard Lafever's unique Corinthian capitals, cast in iron at Janney's Foundry in Montgomery, appeared again. A lighted drum encircled by twelve delicately proportioned Corinthian colonettes support an enlarged dome. The brick building was covered with stucco which was scored to resemble stone, an inexpensive method to simulate the grandeur of marble. In spite of a reduced budget, the builder did incorporate some fine interior detailing. The sweeping spiral staircase dominating the entrance hall was richly carved in fine hardwoods. Columns, recalling a variety of temples and monuments in ancient Greece, adorn the rotunda and support the galleries of the legislative chambers.

The state house was completed in 1851 and was not altered until 1885.

Further additions were made in 1905. Although the Capitol is significant architecturally, its historic association with the organization of the Confederacy had a greater influence on its preservation. The first addition in 1885 appears as a simple extension of the rear wing and precisely copies the proportions and minimal detailing of the Greek Revival structure. Only some interior elements and the Victorian front doors in carved oak and art glass represent the trends of the 1880s.

When the building was enlarged again between 1905 and 1915, the commissioners resisted the temptation to follow the pattern in other states. Instead of tearing down the old building for a newer structure, they planned additions to the north and south wings and improvements for the interior of the older sections. Ambitious plans that would have engulfed the structure in the extravagance of Beaux Arts were rejected for the simple two story additions designed by Montgomery architect Frank Lockwood. Endorsed by the nationally famous New York architect Charles McKim, the Lockwood plans acknowledged a renewed interest in classicisim while leaving the historic portion unchanged and dominant. As in 1885, proportions and details were repeated on the new wings, but they were joined by a narrow enclosed corridor that left the historic legislative chambers intact. The building has now grown as much as it can on Andrew Dexter's optimistically provided site.

FIRST WHITE HOUSE OF THE CONFEDERACY, c. 1833
644 Washington Street

The First White House of the Confederacy was built as a private residence for William Sayre about 1833 by A. M. Bradley, a prominent local contractor. From March to May 1861, after the secession of the Southern states and before the Confederate capital was moved to Richmond, the house was occupied by President Jefferson Davis.

In the 1850s, the house underwent an exterior renovation to conform to the fashionable Italianate style. The colonnade was removed and handsome details including rusticated wood siding under the portico and the iron work "liberty cap" air vents under the eaves were added. The original Federal Period interiors including the trim, wainscot, and mantels were left intact.

In 1920-21, the White House was dismantled and moved from Bibb and Lee Streets to its present location and underwent its first major restoration. In 1976, exterior and interior restoration was undertaken again by Nicholas H. Holmes, architect. Using careful documentation and modern preservation technology, the building was returned to its 1861 appearance.

9. First White House of the Confederacy

In 1877, a group withdrew from the Columbus Street Baptist Church to form the Second Colored Baptist Church of Montgomery. Plans were made to build a permanent home of worship on the corner of Decatur and Dexter Avenues, the former site of a slave trader's pen. Reportedly, masons and carpenters belonging to the newly founded congregation built a temporary frame structure. When the single nave brick church was erected in the 1880s, the congregation changed its name to the Dexter Avenue Baptist Church.

    The cornerstone records P. J. Anderson as the architect. The style of the building is typical of American urban and rural churches. The Gothic Revival was favored for churches during the middle 19th century because of its associations with Gothic churches of the 13th century. In this eclectic building, the Gothic element appears in the pointed arch windows with simplified wooden tracery. The Victorian influence is apparent in the heavily bracketed cornice. Originally, two sets of stairs converged on the main entrance, but they have been replaced by a single, steep concrete stairway.

    The church, the first pulpit of Dr. Martin Luther King, Jr., has been designated a National Historic Landmark.

10. Dexter Avenue Baptist Church

11. *Welcoming the Troops on Commerce Street*

On October 22, 1821, *The Harriet* rounded the bend of the Alabama River, coming into view of the crowds at the foot of Commerce Street. The first steamboat to arrive in Montgomery docked to the cheers of an excited population and inaugurated Commerce Street as the gateway to the city. Soon, travelers and great quantities of goods entered the city along that wide and dusty avenue. Celebrities arrived on sleek riverboats which returned to the port city of Mobile loaded with bales of cotton. Later, fast trains delivered presidents and returning war heroes to the jubilant townsfolk gathered for the occasions.

Two years before *The Harriet's* arrival, Montgomery had been founded by the consolidation of two rival towns. Their adjacent street patterns ran at oblique angles and met at Court Street. The founders of East Alabama, foreseeing the importance of the river, had located the town close to its banks. The founders of New Philadelphia, hoping to catch the travelers coming from Georgia along the Federal Road, had built New Philadelphia on the upper end of Dexter, but with the emergence of rapid river travel, they flocked to Court Square, leaving the upper blocks of Dexter vacant.

Commerce Street, originally part of East Alabama, now connected the new commercial heart of the city with the bustling river front. Cotton warehouses, small brick stores, frame residences, and taverns soon lined the avenue. The first brick structure in town, Freeney's Tavern, was the scene of a ball honoring LaFayette during his 1825 visit to Montgomery. This celebrated event was long preserved in the memories of local ladies who all claimed to have danced with the elderly French hero.

By the 1840s, Montgomery was the thriving trade center for the surrounding countryside. Later, with the completion of the Alabama and West Point Railroad in 1851, it also became a strategic link between port and inland cities. The location of this and later railroads near the river wharf increased the importance of Commerce Street as the transportation center of the city. As a result, grocery wholesalers, formerly on Dexter near Court Square, gravitated toward this district where they remained for the next hundred years.

From the mid 1850s until the turn-of-the-century, trains and riverboats vied for passengers and freight. Large hotels and mercantile establishments displaced homes and taverns along Commerce Street. The new buildings were increasingly elaborate, reflecting the styles which emulated the palaces of Italian merchant princes.

The late 19th century was permeated with the ideas of technology and progress. In 1886, inner-city travel was revolutionized when the world's first electric trolley made its midnight debut on the run from Commerce to Court Square. *The Montgomery Daily Advertiser* noted: "Last night, a street car was seen coming up Commerce minus mules . . ." and it "moved as easily and smoothly as a ghost in the clear moonlight, and at any speed desired." In the same spirit of progress, the present Union Station was erected in 1897 to accommodate the increasing number of passengers entering and leaving the city. Its size, the ambitiousness of the design, and the opulence of the material reflected the importance of rail travel in that day.

Changing methods of transportation and trade in the mid 20th century led to the decline of Commerce Street and the abandonment of many of its buildings. The old tunnel that led under the train tracks to the city wharf is now used as an approach to the new river front park.

12. *Steiner-Lobman Building*

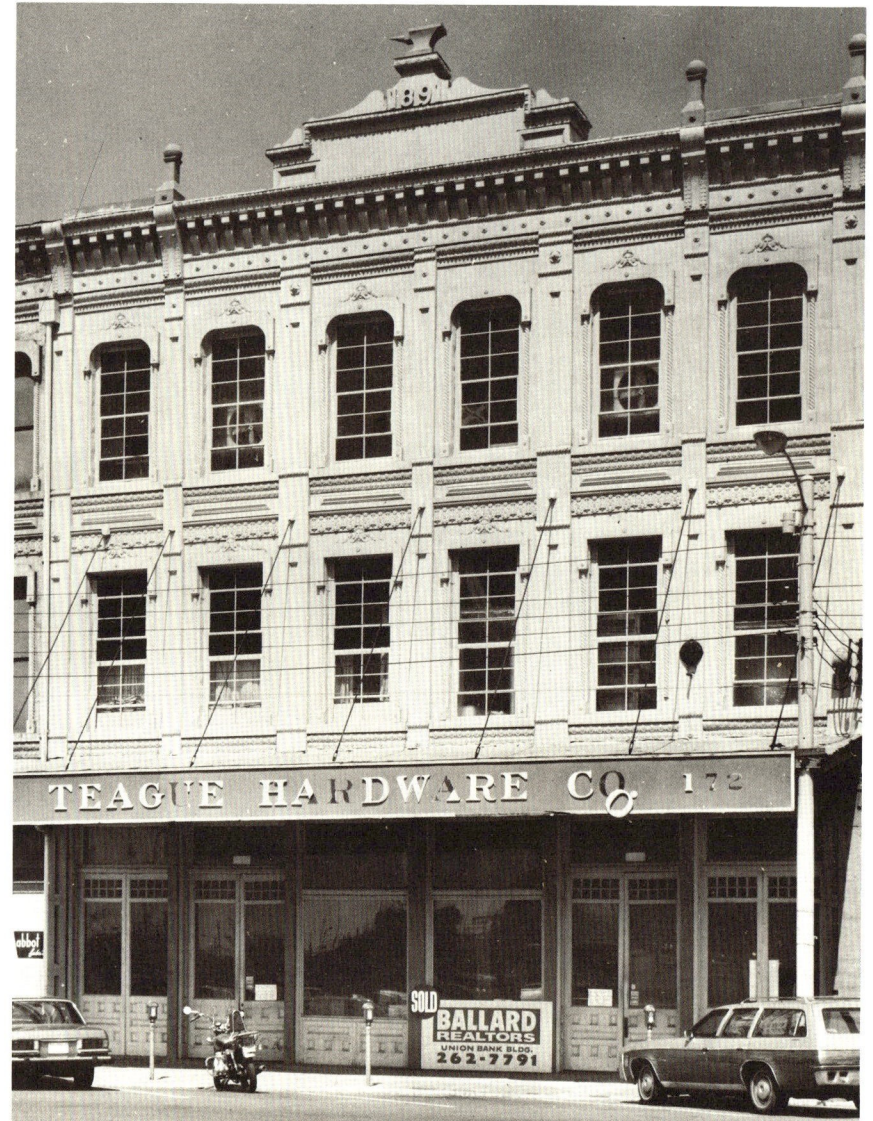

13. *Teague Building*

When Lower Commerce Street underwent a second phase of building in the 1890s and 1900s, major stylistic trends in commercial architecture and building technology were well established. Chicago architects Henry Hobson Richardson and Louis Sullivan had developed new forms suitable to larger buildings. Richardson designed a unique and much copied Romanesque style for commercial and residential structures that initially utilized the continuous horizontal window courses of the popular Italian Renaissance palazzo style, and emphasized a low, rounded arch on the ground floor. Sullivan developed Richardson's style further but with more clean cut, sharply defined surfaces and with vertical groupings under the round arches. As Sullivan moved toward the development of the skyscraper, he began to incorporate structural technology in design by emphasizing support units. Most of these trends are visible in the buildings and warehouses of the Lower Commerce Street area.

Despite these innovations, the more familiar Italian Renaissance design continued as a favorite choice for the prosperous merchants. The wholesale houses, office buildings, and warehouses emulated those of Italy by imitating rusticated stone treatment on the ground floor with tall arched windows or door framing to create an arcade effect. Equal horizontal and vertical window spacing on the upper stories was another characteristic. Windows and rooflines were often ornamented with classically inspired pediments or cornices and terra cotta was used for embellishment.

Technology also played an integral part in design choices. Although the use of cast iron temporarily diminished when the Chicago fire of 1871 proved its inadequate resistance to heat, it continued in use in many small town commercial sections. Street floor cast iron members supported upper story masonry and allowed a greater expanse of glass for display and interior lighting. A variety of metals provided inexpensive facade ornamentation that imitated Italian stone carving. Tin cornices, the most popular form of decoration, can be seen in Montgomery's commercial districts. Most of these buildings also sport a bit of fancy brickwork or a small amount of dressed stone to delineate stories, emphasize corners or arches, or create a suitable frame for the structure's name and date.

The Steiner-Lobman-Teague Building was constructed in 1891 to house two wholesale firms. In March of that year, the *Montgomery Daily Advertiser* described the "new dry goods emporium" as a "beautiful store house." As one of the most ornate structures on the street, it appears to acknowledge the popularity of Renaissance elements while utilizing the technical advances of the period. The front elevation features a ground floor of cast iron pilasters and large plate glass display windows set in wood recesses. The clean cut pilasters give the appearance of stone and suggest Sullivan's influence. The upper stories and roofline of the front and side elevations offer a rich combination of detail, ingenious use of material, and sheer Victorian fancy.

The classical motifs of the stone palazzo are recreated in pressed metal components that sheath the entire masonry portion of the building. Little faces emerge from a swirl of "carving" and peer over each window frame. The metal cornice, one of the most common signatures of the 19th and early 20th century commercial building, features an interesting pierced bracket, perhaps another attempt to imitate carved stone.

The fascination with metal culminates in the fanciful, well-known roof ornaments. Over the Teague portion of the building, an anvil announces the nature of business conducted on the premise. The Victorian mansard roofed tower, supports what is locally known as "the coffin." At one time, the tower and anvil flanked an imposing eight foot metal statue of an ancient goddess.

SCHLOSS AND KAHN WAREHOUSE, c. 1895
116 Coosa Street

In the mid 1890s, the firm of Schloss and Kahn, prosperous wholesale grocers and liquor dealers who occupied what is now the Alden Jones Building, found that they needed additional storage space. The company constructed a warehouse on Coosa Street less than a block from the freight depots of the major railroads.

The two story masonry structure, now owned by Bishop Parker, was designed exclusively for use as a warehouse and thus there are a limited number of windows. Ground floor entrances are set in large arches that were similar to those popularized by Richardson and Sullivan. Like the art conscious Italian merchants they sought to emulate, such men as Schloss and Kahn felt the need to ornament even a back street warehouse. The arched doors and windows have simple, but well-defined moldings similar to those on Union Station giving relief to the otherwise smooth surface. The facade is somewhat divided into three units at the second floor level by two statuary niches with gracefully draped terra cotta goddesses who overlook the bustle and activity beneath them.

14. Schloss and Kahn Warehouse

The firm continued to expand and in 1908, a much larger combination office building and warehouse was built onto a triangular lot at Jefferson and Coosa Streets across from the first warehouse.

In the second structure, there is a more extensive use of stone to mark the stories and windows and to provide a solid foundation and keystones for the arches. Round arched windows and rusticated brickwork on the ground floor indicate the continuing Renaissance influence into the 20th century. The entrance portal with matching rusticated Doric columns in stone reinforces the Italian feeling. Like its neighbors, the building was not complete without its metal cornice.

15. *Schloss and Kahn Building*

16. Great Western Railway Building

A proximity to the numerous railroads accounted for the continued expansion of business in the commercial area. Although passenger traffic was concentrated in the opulent Union Station, freight traffic was handled in several different terminals, only one of which remains. In the fiercely competitive environment of 19th century railroading, mergers were common. Following one such consolidation of lines, the Great Western Railway of Alabama constructed a new terminal.

The two story structure is built almost entirely of brick and attests to the continuing popularity of that material. The pale, lightly glazed brick gives the appearance of dressed stone from a distance. Wide, low arches on the ground floor group the windows and unify the building with the others in the area. Unlike the Schloss and Kahn Warehouse, the freight depot is unornamented. An unusual paired chimney treatment springing from a mid story arch and an escutcheon bearing the company name and date provide the only decoration. The no nonsense structure is a sharp contrast to its rival's elaborate terminal.

17. *Union Station*

Union Station, designed for the Louisville and Nashville Railroad by a noted Montgomery builder B. B. Smith, is a significant testimony to the importance of rail travel at the turn-of-the-century. Completed in 1898, the station was located near the city wharfs and and thriving commercial district and serves to illustrate the importance of transportation to the development of the city.

By 1894, 44 passenger trains were entering the city daily and the present station was planned to accommodate the heavy load. The new station was an elegant statement of the luxury and convenience of train travel and was also a concerted effort on the part of L&N to improve its corporate image. The new plans called for steam heat, electricity, and the best materials available. Slate, marble, oak, Georgia granite, and fine brick were incorporated into the new building which cost $200,000.

The imposing plan consisted of a large main passenger building flanked by two smaller buildings which served for baggage and mail. A 600 foot metal train shed covered the area over the tracks. The main building is symmetrically arranged and divided into five parts. The central portion is dominant and contains the entrance which is richly decorated with small fleur-de-lis. Elaborate stained glass fills many of the windows. The wall surface is enlivened by projecting dormer gables, miniature corbled towers, and finely detailed leafy designs. The interior of the main waiting room has carved oak beams and intricate tile flooring.

Recently the station and shed were designated as National Historic Landmarks. The shed, an important feature of the complex, was termed a museum of 19th century technology. Today, the station, one of two such structures in Alabama, is the focal point of the riverfront area.

018430. PERRY AVENUE MONTGOMERY ALA.

18. Perry Street

The impression Montgomery left on the visitor in the 1940s was that of a quiet town of green trees, fragrant gardens, neat white frame houses, and large mansions. Since then portions of the downtown residential area have vanished, but the original appeal remains in various homes and districts.

From the earliest days, social considerations inspired Montgomery's citizens to build the most fashionable homes they could afford. Log cabins gave way to fine houses with delicate Federal period trim, but few of these remain. It is not, however, for the log cabin, the early houses, or the frontier period that Montgomery and the Deep South are famed. It is the boldly executed Greek Revival mansions of the plantation era that symbolize the region.

The Greek Revival style reached its height in the South in the 1840s and early 1850s as expansion of the cotton system brought wealth to the region. In other parts of the nation, the style has been associated with the common man and rising democracy; in the South, the strongest association has been with the planter class. It was in fact the style of the planters, but the builders of Montgomery's Greek Revival mansions were a diversified group. Though they may have held land, they built their homes in town, close to their major sources of income—commercial enterprises.

Occasionally, architects skilled in the correct use of the style were engaged to design the fine houses of merchants, cotton factors, and bankers, but local builders and carpenters also translated the Greek Revival into houses of all sizes, creating uniquely southern buildings. The mere use of Greek proportions and detailing was often sufficient to satisfy the aspirations of the owner. Even the most modest houses frequently sported a deep entablature and box columns. Many of these carpentry efforts were well-proportioned and well-crafted.

By 1840, much of the nation was abandoning the Greek Revival as new styles came into vogue. The Italian styles, which became widely popular in the 1850s, appeared in Montgomery in the late 1840s, but did not surpass the Greek Revival in popularity until the early part of the next decade. By then, few fine houses were built without the heavily bracketed cornices of the style. Like the Greek Revival, the Italianate appeared in watered-down versions. Often a simple row of brackets and a low veranda were sufficient to give a house the modern look.

In the second half of the 19th century, strict revivalism gave way to an eclectic blending of styles and details drawn from a full range of world architecture. Because of the War and Reconstruction, Montgomery did not feel the full impact of the new styles until the return to prosperity in the 1880s. In 1885, a local editor captured the exuberant and eclectic character of the period when he noted: "Almost all blocks ring with noisy clatter of hammer or mellow music of plane and saw. New houses are almost everywhere, plain cottages, little houses with glass doors and green shutters—pretentious dwellings in Queen Anne and Arabesque and Mooresque and every other 'esque'."

The period is equally well-expressed in the ornate Victorian madness of the brick Kennedy-Sims House. Even the smallest two-room shotgun house decorated with modest amounts of gingerbread reflected the style of the day. It was, however, the one and two story middle-class houses generously ornamented with Victorian trim that made up the bulk of the neat frame houses. Small, asymmetrical cottages, with a gabled front room and small veranda abutting it, became the most common house form for the clerks and shopkeepers of the growing city. It was also adopted by merchants, teachers, and nurses who made up the most prosperous portions of the black community.

Toward the end of the century, the Classical and Colonial styles became popular again. The ornate trim and elaborate color schemes of the Victorian era were abandoned for white paint and classical details. Soon, Neo-Classical and Colonial Revival houses lined the extensions of Perry and Court Streets. The stylistic changes of the ensuing years can be traced in the suburbs as they expanded from downtown to the edge of the city. There, in spite of the radically different lifestyles and economic restraints of today, a fondness for these early historical styles persists.

KNOX HOUSE, c. 1845
411 South Perry Street

SEIBELS-BALL-LANIER HOUSE, c. 1855
407 Adams Avenue

In the 1830s and 1840s, the Greek Revival, the first truly national style, dominated American building. One reason for its widespread popularity was that it symbolized classical values and established a visible kinship between America's fledgling democracy and the democracy of ancient Greece. Although it was based on the temples of ancient Greece, books like Minard Lafever's *Beauties of Modern Architecture* translated and adapted it to fit American domestic and commercial purposes.

The Knox House, an example of Greek Revival designed by Stephen Decatur Button, utilized motifs from Lafever's popular builders' guide. The original house had classical Greek columns and entablature, but the massive triangular pediment, a major feature of the Greek temple, was omitted from the design. Characteristic of Greek Revival were the long windows, rectangular transoms, and sidelights.

William Knox and his family owned the mansion until the late 19th century, but by 1907, it had been converted into the Beauvoir Club. The columns were removed and the interior altered when the now demolished Martha Stuart Apartment Building was constructed around the house.

Samuel Swan began to build one of the finest Italianate mansions in Montgomery in the mid 1850s. In 1858, the nearly completed house was sold for $20,000 to John Jacob Seibels, a native of South Carolina and former Minister to Belgium (1853-55). Seibels, founder of *The Confederation,* a paper supportive of the Union during the pre-Civil War period, joined the Confederate Army at the outbreak of the War. Mary Seibels, John's daughter, married Colonel Charles Pollard Ball, the first Southerner to resign from West Point at the start of the War, and their daughter Mary married Clifford Lanier, the nephew of the poet Sidney Lanier. The house remained in the family for five generations until it was sold to the Scottish Rites Order in the early 1950s.

The Italian influence is evident throughout the two story masonry structure, particularly in the flat cupola with bracketed eaves. A smaller Italianate building which combines brick with board and battan is also located on the grounds and reflects the style of the main house. It is one of the few original slave quarters remaining in Montgomery today. The original carriage house also stands intact at the rear of the building.

19. Knox House

20. Seibels-Ball-Lanier House

MURPHY HOUSE, 1851
22 Bibb Street

The recently restored Murphy House was built for John H. Murphy, a cotton broker and one of the incorporators of Montgomery's first water works. The house served as a center of social activity until the arrival of Union troops in 1865 who used the building as one of their headquarters. Before being restored by the City Water Works Board in 1970, it was occupied by the Elks Club and others for many years.

Compared to the Knox House, details on the 1851 Murphy House are more elaborate. Both structures were built of brick and then stuccoed and scored, and both have an entablature supported by Corinthian columns, but the capitals on the Murphy House columns are more ornate. To add to its opulent appearance, heavy architraves decorate the first floor windows and a smaller version of the portico columns are repeated on either side of the central door.

This house, like the Seibels-Ball-Lanier House, was listed on the Historical American Building Survey, a 1930s WPA survey of architecturally and historically significant landmarks. It is also listed in the National Register of Historic Places which indicates that the federal government regards it as an irreplaceable part of our cultural heritage.

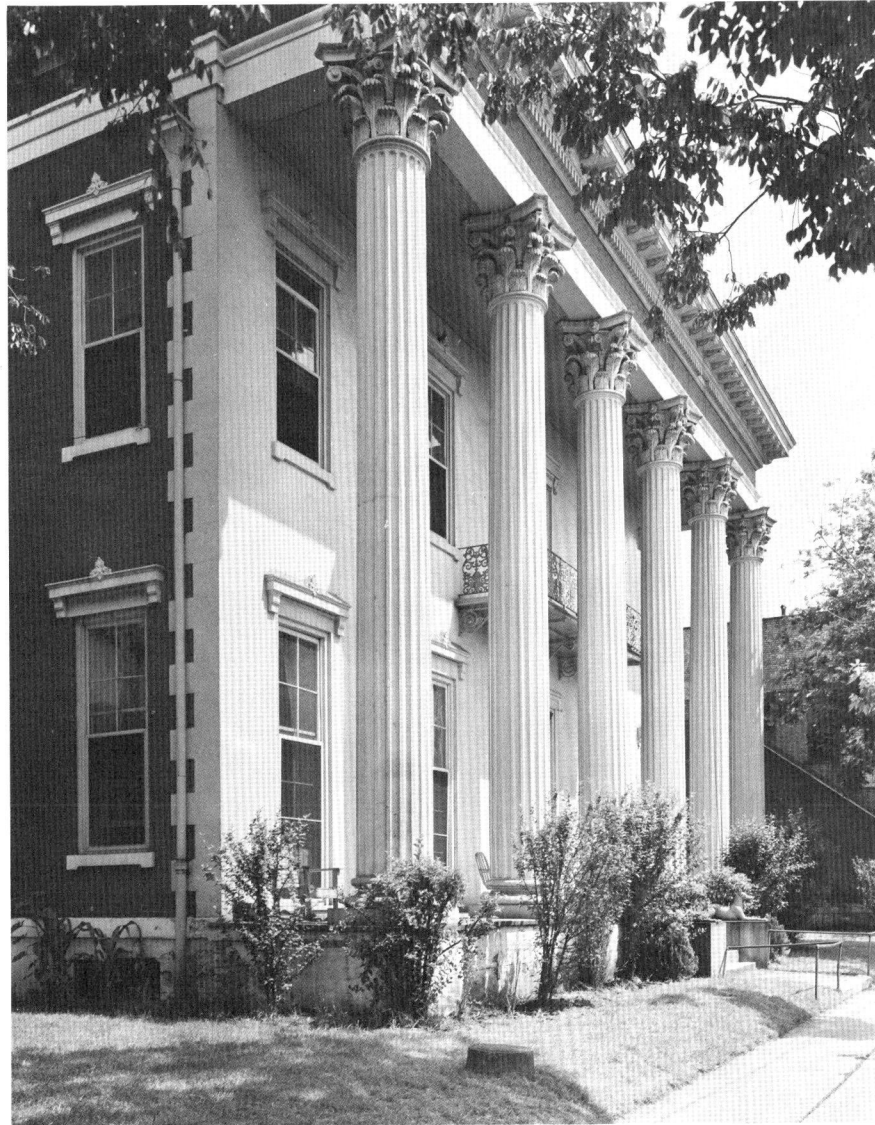

21. Murphy House

JACKSON HOUSE, 1853
409 Union Street

In 1853, Jefferson Franklin Jackson, a prominent Montgomery lawyer and philanthropist, completed this clapboard dwelling. Slight evidence such as the arrangement and types of chimneys suggests that a portion of the house may have been built at an earlier date. This house was appropriately designed for a southern climate and thus has a wide veranda, full-length mirrors that function as doors, and spacious rooms. Because the house was situated on a hill, the front was elevated on brick piers so that the interior floors would be level.

The house combines elements of several building styles. The door trim shows a Greek Revival influence, but the increasingly popular Italianate style is evident in the veranda and bracketed eaves.

Until the 1940s, the Jackson House, with most of its original furnishings, remained in the family. In 1943, it became the community house for the Montgomery City Federation of Women's Clubs. Recently, it has served as a Head Start Center. When the current restoration is completed, the house will be the center of other community services.

22. Jackson House

DOWE HOUSE, c. 1861
334 Washington Avenue

The Dowe house, one of the oldest residences in Montgomery that has been owned and occupied by one family, was possibly the first house of its size in Montgomery to have an inside kitchen and bathroom. Although it seems to be a Greek Revival mansion, its present appearance dates from the 20th century when classical Ionic columns and pediment were added to the front. Like a number of houses in the lower South, it has a ground story of brick and an upper story of wood. Originally, the upper floor served as the main entrance to the house and was reached by a flight of bowlegged stairs. In 1908, the wooden stairs were replaced; later, the present portico was added to give the house a more stylish look.

The additions to the Dowe House reflect the renewed interest at the turn-of-the-century in the classical styles. Throughout Montgomery's history, buildings were commonly updated by altering the facade to conform to the fashion of the day. Recently, however, the trend is to maintain the unique architectural character of older buildings.

23. *Dowe House*

ORDEMAN-SHAW HOUSE, 1848
220 North Hull Street

24. *Ordeman-Shaw House*

The national passion for the Greek Revival began to subside in the 1840s. One critic had complained of the difficulty of distinguishing "between a church, a bank and a hall of justice," while another critic declared that "a dwelling house should look like a dwelling house," not like a Greek temple. The new Italianate style, like the Greek Revival, was popularized in the United States by builders' guides. One such book, *Homestead Architecture* by Samuel Sloan, an architect known in Alabama for Bryce Hospital and the first Winter House, gave practical and aesthetic advice.

When Charles C. Ordeman, a German immigrant, architect, and engineer, built his home, he rejected the still popular Greek Revival for the more fashionable style of the Northeast—the Italianate. Ordeman built other buildings in Montgomery like the nearby 1852 Greek Revival Campbell Cottage and the now demolished 1854 Classical Revival Courthouse. Perhaps Ordeman chose the Italianate for his own home to advertise his sophisticated taste and acquaintance with the latest styles.

The Ordeman House basement, which contains a double dining room, is an unusual feature. The restoration as a house museum by the Landmarks Foundation returned the house and original outbuildings to their mid 19th century state. To achieve an accurate restoration, Landmarks employed a noted architectural archaeologist to determine the original appearance of the main house and location and size of the outbuildings. A specialist in mid 19th century plants was also engaged to assist in the recreation of authentic landscaping. The house, open to the public, illustrates middle-class, urban lifestyles of the period.

The distinctive character of the Gerald-Dowdell-Ashley House, one of the few raised cottages in town, has made it a landmark in the city. The unique flavor is the result of a strong Gulf Coast influence mixed with elements of popular mid 19th century styles.

Like many plantation houses of Louisiana, it has a raised brick basement that serves as a ground floor. This difference of materials is repeated in the porch which has brick piers below and slender posts above. The lower piers are filled with arched lattice work, a common Louisiana feature. The house reflects the Italianate influence in the bracketed cornice, while retaining a Greek Revival doorway and incorporating a bit of Victorian fancy in the gingerbread ornament on the porch.

25. Gerald-Dowdell-Ashley House

MAYOR REESE HOUSE, 1856
360 North Hull Street

BUSH HOUSE, c. 1850
648 Jefferson Street

The Mayor Reese and Bush Houses illustrate the popularity of the Greek Revival style for all types of residences regardless of size. They also share certain characteristics of the style as adapted for the South. The front of these two houses suggest Greek temples; both have full entablatures supported by boxed columns and porticoes recessed under low hipped roofs. Less expensive structures frequently utilized square boxed columns with bands of molding that suggest more costly round columns and their elaborate and expensive capitals.

The Mayor Reese House is Montgomery's finest example of the small Greek Revival house. Further stylistic refinements are a simple but well executed Greek entablature and doorway. The clapboard structure was moved from its original site at the corner of Alabama and Decatur Streets to its present location.

So fashionable was the Greek Revival that it was used for the least expensive houses and occasionally even for barns and outbuildings. The decided Greek Revival character of this small cottage was established by simple bands of molding for the capitals and entablature as well as the window trim. Like many early 19th century houses, the facade of the Bush House was "modernized" later by the addition of Victorian trim. Situated in a once thriving residential neighborhood, this house, which was always sold for under $3,000, belonged to the estate of Jefferson Franklin Jackson whose larger home is also featured in this exhibition.

26. *Mayor Reese House*

27. *Bush House*

In 1906, Montgomery's only example of the Chateauesque style was built for Samuel Sabel, a local businessman. Samuel and his brother Moses constructed and occupied several of the city's most elaborate homes. One house that is now demolished was purchased in 1911 and used as the Governor's Mansion for many years.

The Chateauesque was a later 19th century reinterpretation of 16th century French country chateaus that combined Gothic and Renaissance elements. Richard Morris Hunt, an American architect educated in Paris, popularized the style in the United States.

The steep, pointed roof and pinnacled gables create a complex outline that is reminiscent of the early French chateaus. Graceful pointed arches, a profusion of sinuously carved geometric tracery, and foliated capitals enrich the stone surface. Slightly ominous faces above the elaborate portico flank the central windows of the house. The fine detailing and stonework of this house reflect the Victorian ideals of craftsmanship and beauty.

28. Sabel-Cantey House

29. Detail, Sabel-Cantey House

KENNEDY-SIMS HOUSE, 1894
556 South Perry Street

The late 19th century counterpart to the Greek Revival mansion was the grandiose masonry extravaganza which contrasted strongly with the classical symmetry of the earlier buildings. To imbue a house with character and a sense of the picturesque, architects utilized towers, turrets, and decorative motifs from a panoply of cultures.

J. M. Kennedy was the first owner of this structure. Family history relates that he fulfilled a childhood dream when he drew up the plans and supervised the construction. Born in Scotland in 1853, he joined his father in Montgomery in the 1870s. In 1892, he became the proprietor of his father's building supply store and two years later, completed this house.

The Kennedy-Sims House exemplifies Victorian exuberance. Its wildly eclectic and asymmetrical character is accentuated by a tower with an elongated bell shaped dome topped by a finial. Other eccentric features are the colonettes supporting the portico and the unusual beehive element under the dormer. Lavish stained glass and very fine brickwork complete this monument to Victorian taste.

30. Kennedy-Sims House

This extravagant Victorian brick mansion could only have been built in the late 19th century. The square flat-topped tower recalls the Italian Villa style first popular in the 1850s, but the octagonal bay window, distinctive window framing, and the delicate railing on the roof crests are details featured in the Victorian pattern book. Likewise, the interior of the mansion is highly ornate and Victorian in the slightly asymmetrical floor plan. A renewed interest in the classical is evident in the Ionic columns and pediment of the porch which might have been a later addition or alteration.

A. P. Tyson moved to Montgomery from Lowndesboro and eventually built this Victorian house around 1890. Until recently, the house was owned by the Tyson family— occupied first by A. P. Tyson, then by his daughter Sallie Tyson Maner, and then willed to his grandson Pitt Tyson Maner, Jr.

31. Tyson-Maner House

32. Mrs. John Dowe House

"The finest residence in Montgomery will be open to visitors' inspection Wednesday," noted the *Montgomery Advertiser* in 1885. In fact, the Mrs. John Dowe House was thought to be so exemplary that "a revolution in architecture and workmanship is bound to take place in Montgomery." T. C. Powers, a new builder in the city, was hailed for his ability and taste in constructing an "ornament to the city" in the latest style. This structure was among the first to mark the beginning of new building trends as Montgomery emerged from the economic constraints of the Reconstruction period.

The overall three-dimensional and asymmetrical effect add to its picturesque quality which was so admired in the later 19th century. A notable feature of the house is the fine detailing around the windows. The unusual roof appears to be an attempt to imitate the popular mansard roof. The mansard was associated with the Second Empire style, the national architectural vogue of the 1860s through the 1870s and later.

CASSIMUS HOUSE, 1893
110 Jackson Street

COTTAGE VERNACULAR HOUSE, c. 1886-98
630 Martha Street

In 1888, Speridon Mark Cassimus came to Montgomery from Fano, Corfu with funds provided by his brother and father who was one of the first Greek settlers in Alabama. Speridon assisted in the operation of a fruit store which later became a prosperous wholesale produce business. In 1892, he had saved enough money to begin constructing this house at 110 Jackson Street in one of the fine neighborhoods of the city. More importantly, he was able to return to Greece and bring his family to America. At the same time, he brought back plants native to Greece, such as fig trees, Sparta bushes, and jujube trees which were to flourish in the garden of his new home.

The Cassimus House majestically sits on the crest of a hill rising two blocks above and behind the Capitol. For his house, Cassimus shunned lavish Victorian detailing in favor of more classically inspired trim. The domed front porch is a typical Victorian extravagance. Although the house is now offices, the memory of the original owner is still recalled by the stone slab at the entrance gate on which is elegantly carved the name "S. M. Cassimus."

This typical one story clapboard dwelling was built by the Hugger brothers' firm which later became one of the largest Southeastern construction companies. Occupied by people of modest means, this type of structure was small and utilitarian but embellished with Victorian decoration.

The building has a bay window in front with a decorated gable and adjoining porch, a house form that was extremely common in Alabama from the 1880s to shortly after the turn-of-the-century. The decoration that appears on these homes varies according to the period. In this house, the gable's ornamentation is typical of the 1880s and 1890s. It is similar to earlier gingerbread but is heavier and more three-dimensional.

The Hugger brothers were prolific builders who worked in more than fifteen states during the early 20th century. There are many examples of their domestic work in Cottage Hill; the Jefferson Davis Hotel illustrates one of the Hugger brothers' commercial projects. A Hugger built house opposite this structure was the home of one of the brothers when he first came to Montgomery in the mid 1880s.

33. Cassimus House

34. Cottage Vernacular House

35. L. P. Farley House

37. Jno. C. O'Connell House

38. J. B. Nicrosi House

36. W. H. Thomas House

L. P. FARLEY HOUSE, c. 1890
Demolished

W. H. THOMAS HOUSE, c. 1890
Demolished

JNO. C. O'CONNELL HOUSE, c. 1890
Demolished

J. B. NICROSI HOUSE, c. 1890
Demolished

The Queen Anne Style originated in England in the 1870s and 1880s. Later, the term was used to designate certain eclectic structures that shared common characteristics such as the use of contrasting materials, gabled or hipped roofs, fancy brickwork, turrets, and porches and balconies. Americans first learned of the style via the work of the English architect Richard Norman Shaw, but its later popularity was due to the American architect Henry Hobson Richardson who designed one of the famous Newport summer "cottages," the Watts Sherman House. By the end of the 19th century, distinctively Americanized Queen Anne buildings could be found in large and small cities and towns throughout the United States.

The four houses pictured here— L. P. Farley House, W. H. Thomas House, Jno. C. O'Connell House, and J. B. Nicrosi House—show the diversity of interpretations of the Queen Anne style. Although it could be found in abundance on finer residential streets, few examples remain. These four houses are all demolished.

The L. P. Farley House was the most delicate. Wood was utilized in diverse ways to create a multitude of textures and patterns. Wooden shingles, a distinctively American feature, covered the rounded tower which terminated in a conical tower. Fluted fan-shaped designs were repeated at various points, and web-like spindle ornaments gave a light and airy feeling not found in the other houses. Stained glass and delicate swags and garlands added a richness of surface.

The builder of the W. H. Thomas House eschewed the light and delicate appeal of the Farley House and selected a more dignified and substantial design. A solid appearance achieved by massing of rectangular shapes was relieved by the variety of openings formed by balconies and porches. Wood siding, brick, stone, and shingles provided a strong contrast of surface textures.

Gables, towers, balconies, and chimneys, dominated the Jno. C. O'Connell House, another example of the Queen Anne style. The diverse sizes of the gables and towers created a chaotic and asymmetrical roofline. Balconies and turrets jutted out at the second floor to form a multilayered surface. Restrained classical trim on the wrap-around porch was repeated in the second floor balconies.

The curvilinear Victorian ornament located on the balconies and verandas and bracketed eaves of the J. B. Nicrosi House dressed the surfaces of this otherwise plain building. Roof gables, ornate chimneys, and delicate metal ornament enlivened the roofline. Like the other three houses, the Nicrosi House was built close to the street and its neighbors.

Numerous examples of Queen Anne architecture on narrow city lots once lined the streets of Montgomery and delighted passersby who found similarities and eccentricities in these buildings. The turn-of-the-century fascination with classical styles brought an end to this flamboyant asymmetrical style.

39. Capital

40. Cast iron

Beaux Arts architecture
An architectural style taught at the Ecole des Beaux Arts in Paris in the 19th century that was eclectic, elaborate in design, and generally classically inspired.

Board and batten
Wood construction in which a vertical strip or batten covers the joint between the boards.

Bracket
A supporting member projecting from a wall that is often used for decorative or structural purposes.

Capital
The top decorated part of a column, post or pier.

Cast iron
Iron which has been shaped in a mold.

Classical architecture
The architectural style of ancient Greece or Rome from which later styles were derived. It is often characterized by columns of the classical orders—Doric, Ionic, and Corinthian.

Colonette
A small column that is usually decorative.

Commercial style
An architectural style dating from about 1875 to 1915 used for commercial buildings that is characterized by basically straight fronts, flat roofs, level skylines, and an extensive use of glass.

Corinthian column
A classical column characterized by a capital ornamented with acanthus leaves.

Cornice
The uppermost projecting section of a wall or entablature.

41. Bracketed eaves

42. Escutcheon

Doric column
A classical column characterized by a fluted shaft and simple capital consisting of a curved molding beneath a square block.

Dormer window
A window with sides and front that usually projects from a sloping roof.

Eaves
The projecting edge of a roof that overhangs the top of a wall.

Eclectic
Composed of elements drawn from various styles.

Entablature
In classical architecture, the horizontal part of a structure between the column and the roof or pediment which is supported by columns or pilasters.

Escutcheon
An ornamental and usually shield-shaped form on which a coat-of-arms is inscribed.

43. *Finial*

44. *Gingerbread*

Facade
The front part of a building but sometimes other sides given special architectural treatment.

Federal
Architecture of the period c. 1790-1830 that was characterized in Alabama by simple, rectangular structures with delicate woodwork.

Finial
A small crowning ornament atop a gable or spire.

Gable
A triangular-shaped element at the end of a building having a double sloping roof.

Gingerbread
Decorative woodwork made with a scroll saw.

Gothic Revival
An architectural style popular in the United States in the mid 19th century that revived certain forms of 12th through 16th centuries European Gothic architecture. It was characterized by pointed arches, steep gabled roofs, and leaded stained glass.

Greek Revival
An architectural style of the early mid 19th century that was based on architectural forms of ancient Greece and was characterized by the use of classical details and symmetrical forms.

Hipped roof
A roof with slopes on all four sides. The hips are the external angles where an end and side slope meet.

Ionic column
A classical column characterized by a capital with volutes (a spiral scroll).

45. *Keystone*

46. *Masonry*

Italianate

An architectural style popular in the United States in the 1840s and 1850s that was based on the country houses of Italy and Renaissance palaces. It was characterized by bracketed roofs, square towers, and round arched windows.

Keystone

The central wedge-shaped stone of the arch.

Mansard roof

A roof having two slopes on all four sides with a steep lower slope and a flatter upper slope.

Masonry

A structure or object made of stones or brick.

Pediment

In classical style architecture, a triangular space formed by the slope of a gabled roof and a horizontal element beneath it.

47. *Pediment*

48. *Pilaster*

Pier

An upright structure of masonry which serves as a support for beams and arches.

Pilaster

A flat pier attached directly to a wall.

Portico

A porch with a roof supported by columns and usually completed with a pediment.

Queen Anne style

A variant of Victorian architecture named after Queen Anne that was popular in America in the late 19th century. It was characterized by the use of contrasting materials, fancy brickwork, and gabled or hipped roofs.

Raised cottage

A cottage which has its main entrance on the second floor.

Romanesque Revival
An architectural style of the second half of the 19th century that incorporated forms of 11th century Romanesque architecture and was characterized by the round arch.

Rusticated
Stonework in which each stone is separated from the other by a deep joint.

Scored
A stucco finish made to look like stone construction.

Second Empire
An architectural style named after the Second Empire of Napoleon III (1852-70) that was popular in the United States in the 1860s and 1870s and was characterized by its eclecticism and mansard roof.

Shotgun
A traditional folk house consisting of rooms in a straight line.

49. Sidelights and transom

Sidelight
A framed area of glass on either side of a door or window.

Stucco
A mixture of portland cement, lime, sand, and water that is used as an exterior finish or for interior decorative work or moldings.

Transom
A horizontal, glassed area above a window or door.

Turret
A small tower at the corner of a building.

Victorian architecture
A group of architectural styles named after the reign of Queen Victoria (1837-1901) that was popular in the United States in the later 19th century and was characterized by asymmetrical shapes and eclecticism.

50. Turret

This catalog was designed by Julie and Lou Toffaletti, Montgomery, Alabama.

Two thousand copies were produced by Walker printing, Incorporated, Montgomery, Alabama, for the Montgomery Museum of Fine Arts in May of 1978.

The type face used is palatino, set by Composit, Incorporated, Montgomery, Alabama.

The cover stock is Simpson Lee's 80 lb. Corsican cover. The inside stock is 80 lb. Corsican Text.

51. *Freeney's Tavern*